Summer

Signs of the Season
Around North America

Written by Valerie J. Gerard   Illustrated by Jeremy Schultz

Content Advisor: Julie Dunlap, Ph.D. • Reading Advisor: Lauren A. Liang, M.A.
Literacy Education, University of Minnesota, Minneapolis, Minnesota

PICTURE WINDOW BOOKS
MINNEAPOLIS, MINNESOTA

To Hoddy and Charlotte—V.J.G.

Editor: Nadia Higgins
Designer: Melissa Voda
Page production: The Design Lab
The illustrations in this book were prepared digitally.

Picture Window Books
5115 Excelsior Boulevard
Suite 232
Minneapolis, MN 55416
1-877-845-8392
www.picturewindowbooks.com

Printed in the United States of America.

Library of Congress Cataloging-in-Publication Data
Gerard, Valerie J., 1959–
  Summer : signs of the season around North America / written by
Valerie J. Gerard ; illustrated by Jeremy Schultz.
    p. cm. — (Through the seasons) Includes index.
  Summary: Examines how summer brings observable changes in
weather, nature, and people.
  ISBN 1-4048-0003-4 (library binding : alk. Paper
  1. Summer—North America—Juvenile literature. [1. Summer.] I.
Schultz, Jeremy, ill. II. Title. III. Through the seasons (Minneapolis,
Minn.)
  QB637.6 .G47 2003
  508.2—dc21   2002005843

One way to mark the seasons is by looking at the calendar. The calendar dates are based on Earth's yearly trip around the sun. In North America, summer begins on the longest day of the year, either June 20, 21, or 22. Throughout the summer, the days keep getting shorter.

Another way to mark the seasons is to look around you at the changes in weather and nature. In North America, the first signs of summer appear in the south, then move north. This book helps you to see the signs of summer in different places around North America.

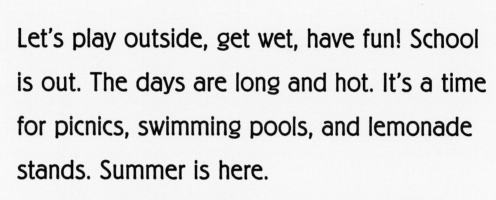

Let's play outside, get wet, have fun! School is out. The days are long and hot. It's a time for picnics, swimming pools, and lemonade stands. Summer is here.

Summer isn't the same everywhere in North America. What happens in summer where you live?

Look in the back for a summer activity.

The desert air is cool early in the summer morning. Coyotes, lizards, and snakes are busy looking for food. Soon the blistering heat will send them to their shady shelters.

Keep your sandals on! The sidewalks are too hot for bare feet.
Swimming pools and fresh lemonade will cool you down.

FUN FACT:
On summer afternoons, heavy
thunderstorms blow into the desert.
They might only last a few minutes, but
they return each day for several weeks.

In the Appalachian Mountains, the air feels thick. Clothes stick to your skin.

FUN FACT:

In the mountains, you might hear a loud buzzing sound coming from the trees. That sound is made by cicadas. The large insects are calling to one another.

In the wilderness, turtles, frogs, and alligators soak up the summer sun.

In California, the beach is the place for summer fun. Children shout and laugh as they try to outrun the booming waves. They take a break in the shade of a colorful umbrella.

Sea birds hover high above, looking for fish in the water. They dive into the ocean for their meal.

In late summer, the corn grows high over your head on a midwestern farm. Calves, lambs, puppies, ducklings, and chicks—all the babies are growing.

10

Mmmmm. The peppers, cucumbers,
and tomatoes are fresh from the garden.
Ice-cream cones drip in the hot sun.

FUN FACT:

Corn grows as much as an inch (2 ½ centimeters)
in one day. By the end of the summer, it has grown
seven feet (two meters) tall.

At night, fireflies twinkle in the tall grass.

Their little lights seem to dance with the stars.

The air stays hot all night. Mosquitoes buzz in your ear.
Crickets and frogs are calling outside.

In summer, tourists wander the streets of New England's oldest towns. Family and friends gather on the beach for clambakes and bonfires. Sailboats float in the distance.

On the horizon, dark clouds form.

A storm is approaching.

Rat-tat-tat! Boom-boom-boom! Hear the marching band's drums? Look at the fire truck rumbling down the street. The parade is coming!

It's getting dark. Spread out your blanket for fireworks.
The cool grass tickles your toes.

Get out your hiking boots, bug spray, and binoculars! In summer, there is plenty of daylight for exploring nature in Alaska and northern Canada. The sun stays bright long into the night.

FUN FACT:
In Barrow, Alaska, the sun does not set for 84 days. It rises in May and does not go down until August. Because the summer sun can be seen all night, it is called the midnight sun.

Fish swim upriver to lay their eggs. Hungry bears wait along the riverbanks. Young birds stretch their wings, preparing to fly. By the end of summer, they must be ready for their journey south.

19

Now you know what summer is like in different places in North America. What happens in summer where you live?

FUN FACT:

In summer, towns celebrate special days with festivals, fairs, and outdoor concerts. On July 1st, people celebrate Canada Day with fireworks and parades. The United States celebrates its birthday on the Fourth of July. Labor Day signals the end of summer vacation, when it's time to go back to school.

DESERTS

Nogales, Mexico

Average high June temperature: 94°F/34°C

Hours of daylight on June 21st: 14 hours, 11 minutes

What to wear: shorts, sandals, hat, sunglasses

Signs of summer: lemonade and sunscreen lotion

APPALACHIAN MOUNTAINS

Asheville, North Carolina

Average high June temperature: 80°F/27°C

Hours of daylight on June 21st: 14 hours, 34 minutes

What to wear: sleeveless shirt, skirt or shorts, hat

Sign of summer: sticky, humid air

CALIFORNIA COAST

San Diego, California

Average high June temperature: 71°F/22°C

Hours of daylight on June 21st: 14 hours, 19 minutes

What to wear: bathing suit

Sign of summer: beach umbrellas

MIDWEST

St. Louis, Missouri

Average high June temperature: 85°F/29°C

Hours of daylight on June 21st: 14 hours, 52 minutes

What to wear: shorts, T-shirt, sneakers

Sign of summer: corn

NEW ENGLAND

Portsmouth, New Hampshire

Average high June temperature: 76°F/24°C

Hours of daylight on June 21st: 15 hours, 23 minutes

What to wear: shorts or skirt, T-shirt

Sign of summer: tourists

ALASKA/NORTHERN CANADA

Anchorage, Alaska

Average high June temperature: 61°F/16°C

Hours of daylight on June 21st: 19 hours, 22 minutes

What to wear: light sweater

Sign of summer: salmon

Make an Ice Cube Sailboat

You Will Need:

Water

An ice cube tray

Toothpicks

Tape

Tissue paper or other lightweight paper

Fill an ice cube tray with water. Put a piece of tape over the rows of cubes so that each section has tape going over it. Poke toothpicks through the tape and into the water in each section. Place the tray in the freezer. The toothpicks will freeze in place. Meanwhile, cut several 1-inch (2 $\frac{1}{2}$-centimeter) triangles from the lightweight paper, one for every cube. Once the ice cubes are frozen, remove them from the tray. Pierce the paper triangle with the toothpick to make a sail. Then send your sailboats off on a race across a kiddie pool or bathtub.

Words to Know

Canada Day—a Canadian holiday that honors the day in 1867 when Canada was united to become the country it is today. Canada Day is July 1.

Fourth of July—a U.S. holiday, also called Independence Day. People celebrate America's birthday, when the colonies declared their independence from England in 1776.

Labor Day—a U.S. holiday to honor people who work. Labor Day falls on the first Monday in September.

midnight sun—when the sun is out all day and night. Midnight sun happens in summer at the far northern and southern parts of Earth.

summer—the season between spring and autumn. Summer lasts from the end of June to the end of September.

To Learn More

AT THE LIBRARY

Dotlich, Rebecca Kai. *Lemonade Sun: And Other Summer Poems.* Honesdale, Pa.:
  Wordsong/Boyds Mills Press, 1998.

Gibbons, Gail. *The Reasons for Seasons.* New York: Holiday House, 1995.

Jackson, Ellen B. *The Summer Solstice.* Brookfield, Conn.: Millbrook Press, 2001.

Stille, Darlene R. *Summer.* Minneapolis: Compass Point Books, 2001.

FACT HOUND

Fact Hound offers a safe, fun way to find Web sites related to this book. All of the sites on Fact Hound have been researched by our staff.

http://www.facthound.com

1. Visit the Fact Hound home page.
2. Enter a search word related to this book, or type in this special code: 1404800034
3. Click the FETCH IT button.

Your trusty Fact Hound will fetch the best sites for you!

Index